The 71 Quarter Circle Ranch Headquarters:
A Report

Zoe Jane Carmina

Discover other titles by Zoe Carmina on Amazon!
amazon.com/author/zoecarmina

I0412458

Paperback Edition, License Notes

ABSTRACT

The 71 Quarter Circle Ranch was founded by a wealthy Nebraska cattleman named John Stewart during the 1870s, and was later acquired by a Scottish consortium whose manager, John Clay, was President of the Wyoming Stock Growers Association during the range wars. Located just downstream from Three Crossings, the original headquarters complex of barns, corrals, and cabins was built on the north side of the river. In the early 1880s, new buildings were erected on the south side.

Surface evidence at these two sites suggests markedly different "levels of settlement" that do not agree with written accounts. In addition, there is considerable evidence of illegal fencing predating the small homesteaders' fences which so enraged the cattle barons, and was used as partial justification for their assaults on small ranchers.

INTRODUCTION

This paper was produced as part of the Central Wyoming College "Middle Sweetwater Archaeological Project." The CWC Western American Studies Program received a research grant from the National Park Service—Long Distance Trails Office, to locate and document Oregon-California Trail-related archaeological sites along the Middle and Upper Sweetwater. Archaeological investigations were conducted primarily during April, May, and June of 2010.

The project did not involve an intensive, Class III survey. Project directors had casually observed many prehistoric and historic sites in the area while working on other endeavors since the 1980s. During the 2010 field season over 50 previously undocumented sites and trail segments were recorded, and about 10 previously recorded sites were recorded again in greater detail than the original reports.

Individual prehistoric cairns, firepits, and small Lithic scatters, all of which are numerous, were not recorded. Historic sites including military posts, stage and Pony Express stations, trail ruts, telegraph stations, homesteads, and road ranches were recorded.

AREA DESCRIPTION

The 71 Ranch Headquarters are located about a mile downstream from the Three Crossings Stage Station in the Sweetwater Valley. The sites are situated on both sides of the Sweetwater River in the grassy riparian. The grassy riparian area changes to dry grasses, sage brush, and prickly pear habitat.

The site is bounded on the south by a very sandy embankment, created of sand dunes. Portions of the 2nd Crossing of the Sweetwater are likely located near these sites. There are also Pre-1883, Rongis to Lost Cabin Wagon Road ruts, running north to south through both sites.

These sites are currently being utilized as a livestock and cattle range as well as a natural habitat, but they are closed to the public by the landowner, Western Nuclear.

HISTORICAL DATA

This ranch land originated as John Stewart's '71 Quarter Circle Ranch' which was bought in 1882 from Stewart by John Clay on behalf of a Scottish Syndicate, calling themselves the Wyoming Cattle Ranche Company. The new owners decided to dismantle the original buildings and build a new complex to the South of the river.

Surface evidence at these two sites suggests markedly different "levels of settlement." The 1st 71 Ranch appears to have been very basic, while the 2nd 71 Ranch was much more elaborate, with many more buildings, and a greater amount of trash deposits.

DESCRIPTION OF SITES

The 71 Quarter Circle Ranch Headquarters sites are both multi-component sites. They each contain Prehistoric Lithic Scatter and encompass the Pre-Territorial, Territorial, and Expansion periods which range from 1842 through 1928.

DESCRIPTION OF FEATURES AND ARTIFACTS

The 1st 71 Ranch is the 1879 John Stewart 71 Quarter Circle Ranch. There is a cabin or blacksmith shop foundation, or combination building with fireplace remnants. About 35 unshaped granite rocks 20-30 centimeters in size serve as the foundation for this shop. Over 20 rusted metal pieces are scattered near this foundation, along with an unidentified burned material, a modified wagon seat piece, and a few burned slag pieces from a forge.

There are possible remains of a 2nd building foundation, with about a 10 stone concentration, in which two rocks appear to have mortar on them. This rock group measures about 1.5 meters in diameter.

There is a log fenced area, with no gate, 3 meters square with pine poles and pine rails, 1.4 meters high. At least one square nail adorns the structure as well as other wire nails.

Other artifacts at the site of the 1st 71 Ranch include a wagon axle piece made of iron, about 13 or more pieces of transcontinental telegraph wire, and an iron cinch ring. This 1st 71 Ranch Headquarters was only occupied about 5 to 10 years, from the mid-1870s to 1882.

The 2nd 71 Ranch is the John Clay 71 Quarter Circle Ranch. There is a cabin foundation depression with berm, which measures 12 meters East to West by 11.5 meters North to South. The berm measures up to 1.5 meters high on the south and west sides, and down to 0.7 meters high on the north and east sides.

Next to the building are ruts of the Oregon Trail as well as ruts of the Pre-1883 Rongis to Lost Cabin Wagon Road. There is a large hay corral on the site, as well as a charcoal stain of unknown date in the Oregon Trail ruts.

Artifacts at the site of the 2nd 71 Ranch are much more numerous. Three different types of haying equipment representing different time frames were found, one of which was part of a horse drawn haying mower, with a McCormick 1878 patent date.

Numerous pieces of wire, transcontinental telegraph wire, as well as hand-crimped telegraph wire were found.

A number of cartridges were found on the site. Some of these cartridges appeared to be split longitudinally, which happens when a bullet is shot from a gun that it's not made for. This can sometimes be interpreted as a sign that there was a Native American occupation in the area, as they would frequently use whatever bullets they could find in their guns.

Numerous miscellaneous artifacts were also found, including ceramic fragments, a possible electrical object, fragments of a portable iron stove, a gold ink pen nib, a horseshoe, a door latch, a tin can piece with 'Chicago' and 'Omaha' on the can, and a woman's wire garter holder. A brown glass bottle base which was manufactured between 1877 and 1909 by Burlington Glass [Works] Company was also found, along with a saw medallion sporting the label 'H. Disston & Sons, Philadelphia', and manufactured during the 1880s. The 2nd 71 Ranch Headquarters is much more significant in terms of its association with people and events.

DISCUSSION

Historical evidence says that the 1st 71 Quarter Circle Ranch Headquarters complex of barns, corrals, and cabins was built on the north side of the river, and was located just downstream from the Three Crossings. This is evidenced at the site with the foundation of a cabin or blacksmith shop, or combination building with fireplace remnants, as well as the possible remains of a 2nd building foundation, and a log fenced area, with no gate, made of pine poles and pine rails.

The burned materials, burned slag, and modified wagon seat piece discovered near the first foundation make it very likely the structure was a repair shop that dealt in metalworking. There is also other surface evidence of habitation.

At the 2nd 71 Ranch location there is considerable evidence of illegal fencing predating the small homesteaders' fences, which so enraged the cattle barons, and was used as partial justification for their assaults on small ranchers. The hand-crimped transcontinental telegraph wire, modified to be Kennedy Star barbed wire, is evidence that such illegal fencing activity was going on at the 71 Ranch.

When John Stewart bought the Three Crossings area, there were miles of transcontinental telegraph wire being stored on the site. Stewart employed his cowboys one winter, hand-crimping the barbs on the telegraph wire which they then used to fence off thousands of acres of Sweetwater river bottom. These illegal fencing ventures by smaller ranching operations eventually lead to the brutal Johnson County War.

John Clay, who at the time was both the manager of the 71 Quarter Circle Ranch, and the President of the Wyoming Stock Growers Association, was suspected of playing a major role in the bringing about of the Johnson County War, which he later denied. He did however, help the Wyoming Stock Growers Association and their associates from avoiding punishment after their surrender.

CONCLUSION

The 71 Quarter Circle Ranch Headquarters, is in a prime location just downstream from the Three Crossings Stage Station, near the possible 2nd Crossing of the beautiful Sweetwater River, and right next to the Oregon Trail. This important ranch became one of the largest ranches in all of Wyoming, and the success of the 71 Quarter Circle Ranch helped to inspire the National cattle boom of the 1880s. It is an important place to the history of Wyoming, and it is tucked away in Fremont County, right in our own backyard.

If you enjoyed this piece, you can discover other titles by Zoe Carmina by visiting her on the web. Zoe Carmina thanks you very much for your support!

Amazon:
amazon.com/author/zoecarmina

Facebook:
https://www.facebook.com/zoejanecarmina/